Let's Look at the Seasons
Springtime

By Ann Schweninger

Viking

The art was prepared with graphite pencil,
colored pencil, and watercolor paint on
Arches 90-pound cold-press watercolor paper.

VIKING
Published by the Penguin Group
Penguin Books USA Inc., 375 Hudson Street, New York, New York 10014, U.S.A.
Penguin Books Ltd, 27 Wrights Lane, London W8 5TZ, England
Penguin Books Australia Ltd, Ringwood, Victoria, Australia
Penguin Books Canada Ltd, 10 Alcorn Avenue, Toronto, Ontario, Canada M4V 3B2
Penguin Books (N.Z.) Ltd, 182–190 Wairau Road, Auckland 10, New Zealand

Penguin Books Ltd, Registered Offices: Harmondsworth, Middlesex, England

First published in 1993 by Viking, a division of Penguin Books USA Inc.

1   3   5   7   9   10   8   6   4   2

Library of Congress Cataloging-in-Publication Data
Schweninger, Ann. Springtime / by Ann Schweninger.
p.   cm.—(Let's look at the seasons)
Summary: Text and activities introduce the natural wonders of springtime.
I S B N 0 - 6 7 0 - 8 2 7 5 7 - 6
1. Spring—Juvenile literature.   2. Nature study—Juvenile
literature.   [1. Spring.   2. Nature study.]   I. Title.
II. Series: Schweninger, Ann. Let's look at the seasons.
QH81.S385 1993   574.5′43—dc20   92-22204 CIP AC

Printed in Mexico   Set in ITC Cheltenham Light

For Cecilia Yung

First Day

The first day of spring is usually March 20th.

I'm tired of playing indoors.

As spring arrives, there is more daylight. And slowly days will grow warmer, too. But early spring can be cold.

Spring Fever

Wintry weather has been here for months. We long for the freedom springtime brings. This feeling is called spring fever.

Early Spring

Crocuses are blooming. And underground, daffodil shoots are pushing up toward the earth's surface.

Leaf buds on trees and bushes are swelling, about to unfold.

Overhead, flocks of robins and Canada geese return north. They spent the winter in warmer climates where food was easier to find.

April Fools' Day

April Showers

High in the air, tiny particles of water—so tiny they cannot be seen—collect on specks of dust and form water droplets. The droplets move along together, becoming clouds. In warm clouds, the water droplets bump into each other again and again. They merge, growing into bigger and bigger droplets. At last they are too heavy to stay in the air. And they fall to earth as rain.

Planting Seeds

You can begin a garden indoors. Here's what you need:

seeds

empty cardboard egg cartons

potting soil

newspaper

scissors

tape

water

aluminum foil

or old plates

Spread newspaper over your work area. Then cut the lids off the egg cartons.

Fill each egg holder with soil.

Put a seed in each holder. The seed package tells how deep to plant it.

Tape the seed package (back side out, so you can see the instructions) to the carton.

Very gently, water the seeds.

Set each carton on a piece of aluminum foil or an old plate in a warm, sunny place indoors.

Don't let the soil become too dry.

The seed package will tell you how long it will be before the seeds sprout.

As the seedlings grow, watch them lean toward the sun.

When the seedlings are a few inches tall, it will be time to transplant them outside in the garden soil or, if you live in an apartment, into plant pots.

What Makes Gardens Grow?

What makes gardens grow?

Warmth and energy come from the sun.

Moisture comes from rain.

Pull weeds that would crowd crops.

Put up fences and scarecrows to keep out animals that might eat crops.

When the soil is dry, water it.

Hoe to loosen the soil so air reaches plant roots.

I picked flowers for you!

Thanks!

Enrich the soil with fertilizer so plants grow strong and big.

Read books to learn about gardening.

Baseball

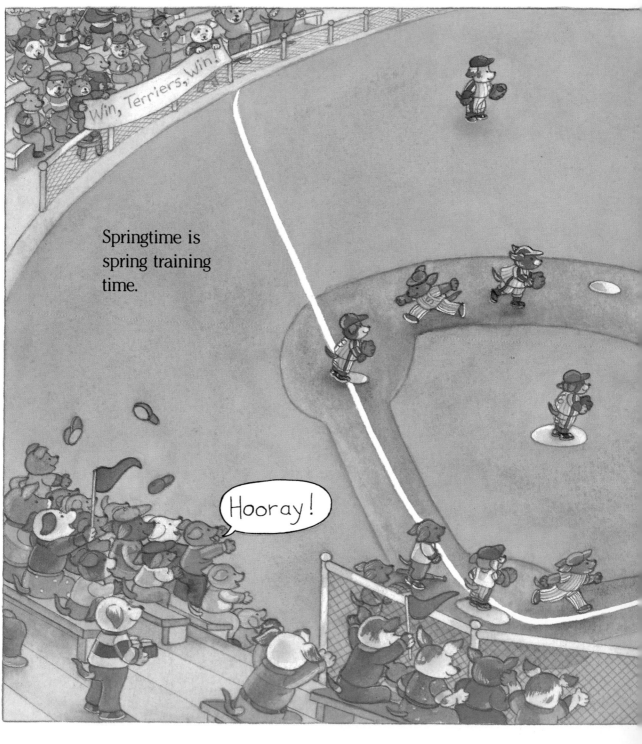

Springtime is spring training time.

Hooray!

Take out the balls,
mitts, bats, and caps!

It's Opening Day!
Time to cheer!
Time to play!

Spring Flowers

March

crocus

April

daffodil

forsythia

pussy willow

May

tulip

lilac

cherry blossom

June

rose

iris

peony

Baby Animals

Spring is a time of birth and of growth. Baby animals are born now, when it is warm, when food is plentiful, and when they will have all summer to grow and prepare for winter.

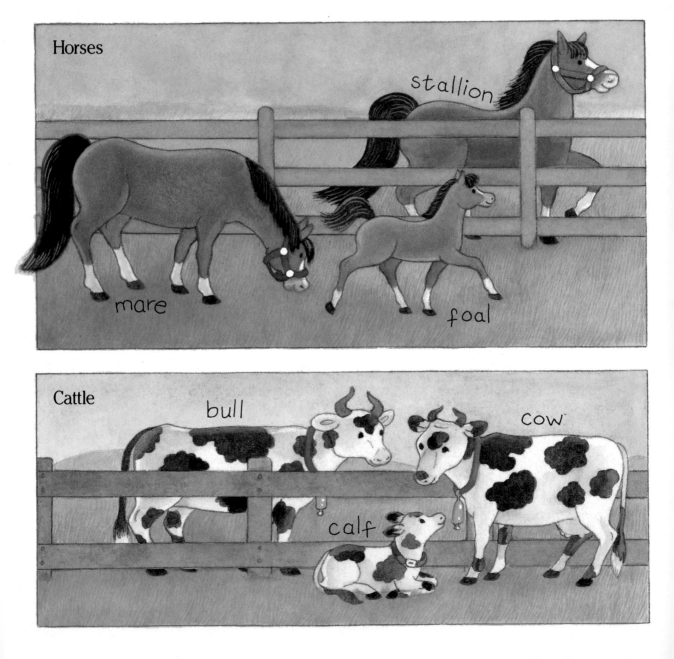

Pigs

hog

sow

piglets

Sheep

ram

ewe

lamb

Geese

gander

goslings

goose

Rabbits

buck

doe

fawns

Spring Eggs

To keep them warm, a mother robin sits on her clutch of eggs.

About two weeks after they are laid, it's time for the eggs to hatch.

Parent birds feed their nestlings insects and worms.

After about two weeks, baby birds, now called fledglings, leave the nest and learn to fly. For about a month, their parents continue to guard and to feed them.

Robins

Frogs

Frog eggs are incubating in warm, shallow pond water, where their mother laid them.

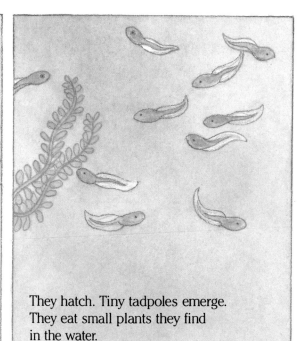

They hatch. Tiny tadpoles emerge. They eat small plants they find in the water.

As tadpoles grow larger, they develop legs and lungs.

Then their tails are absorbed into their bodies.
Tadpoles become frogs.

Looking Inside a Tulip Blossom

anther   stigma   style

The smell and bright color of a tulip blossom attract insects which gather nectar for food from inside the blossom.

Inside the petals, the anther holds pollen, a fine yellow powder that rubs onto insects. As they move from tulip to tulip, the pollen rubs off onto one tulip, then another.

The pollen sticks to the stigma, then grows down through the style, where it enters an ovule. Now the ovule will grow into a seed. And the seed can grow into a new plant.

Field Day

The school year is almost over. Summer vacation begins soon. But now it is time for Field Day.

Late Spring

Baby woodchucks snuggle in an underground nursery. Soon they will come out to munch on grass and clover.

Young chipmunks explore near the entrance to their underground den. They look for seeds and strawberries to eat.

Baby squirrels have left the tree hollow where they were born. They skitter along branches, where they find leaves, buds, nuts, and insects to eat.

Tiny cottontail rabbits are hidden in a shallow nest their mother dug and lined with dry leaves, grass, and her own soft fur.

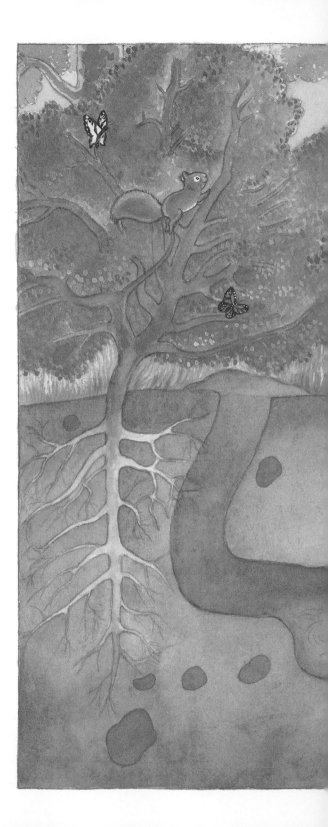

June

As spring ends, warm days are filled with sunlight and sound.

Bees buzz.

Birds chirp, warble, and sing.

Musicians fiddle, strum, and toot.

Skateboards glide.

Children shout.

Breezes rattle leaves on trees.

Hummingbirds hum.

And a lawn mower roars.